D1120299

Mighty Machines
DIGGERS

Amanda Askew

WITHDRAWN

QEB Publishing

Words in **bold** can be found
in the Glossary on page 23.

Copyright © QEB Publishing, Inc. 2010

Published in the United States by
QEB Publishing, Inc.
3 Wrigley, Suite A
Irvine, CA 92618

www.qed-publishing.co.uk

All rights reserved. No part of this publication may be reproduced, stored in
a retrieval system, or transmitted in any form or by any means, electronic,
mechanical, photocopying, recording, or otherwise, without the prior permission
of the publisher, nor be otherwise circulated in any form of binding or cover
other than that in which it is published and without a similar condition being
imposed on the subsequent purchaser.

A CIP record for this book is available from the Library of Congress.

ISBN 978 1 59566 926 1

Printed in the United States

Written by Amanda Askew
Designed by Phil and Traci Morash (Fineline Studios)
Editor Angela Royston
Picture Researcher Maria Joannou

Picture credits
Key: t = top, b = bottom, c = center, FC = front cover, BC = back cover

Alamy Images David Williams 17c, Mike Dobel 18–19, David R. Frazier
Photolibrary Inc 21t; **Dreamstime** Grazvydas 1, 6–7; **Getty Images** Liam
Bailey 14b, 22br; **Istockphoto** Purdue9394 4–5, Shaun Dodds 12, Sascha
Rosenau Njaa 14–15, Shaun Dodds 22tr; **Photolibrary** Age Fotostock/Gary
Moon 9b, 22bl, Tips Italia/Bildagentur RM 10–11, Index Stock Imagery/Bill
Keefrey 11t, Age Fotostock/ Javier Larrea 13, Imagebroker.net/Jochen Tack
20–21, Tips Italia/Bildagentur RM 22tl; **Shutterstock** mg14008 FC, Sevda
4, Stanislav Komogorov 6, Jiri Slama 8–9, 22tc, GRAPIX BC; **U Mole** 16–17,
22bc (Photos supplied by **U Mole**, a division of VP plc detailing MTS suction
excavation equipment. For more info visit www.umole.co.uk)

Contents

What is a digger?

A digger digs holes and trenches. Diggers are also called excavators. These machines are often used on **building sites**, with **loaders** and **bulldozers**.

A digger on wheels can go on the road to get from one job to another.

Some diggers have big wheels. Other diggers run on tracks. Tracks stop the digger from sinking into the ground.

A digger with tracks is called a crawler. It can move over rough ground.

tracks

Parts of a digger

A digger has three main parts—a cab, an arm, and an **attachment**. The attachment is usually a **bucket** with teeth. The bucket scoops up the soil and stones.

The driver sits in the cab and controls the digger.

tracks

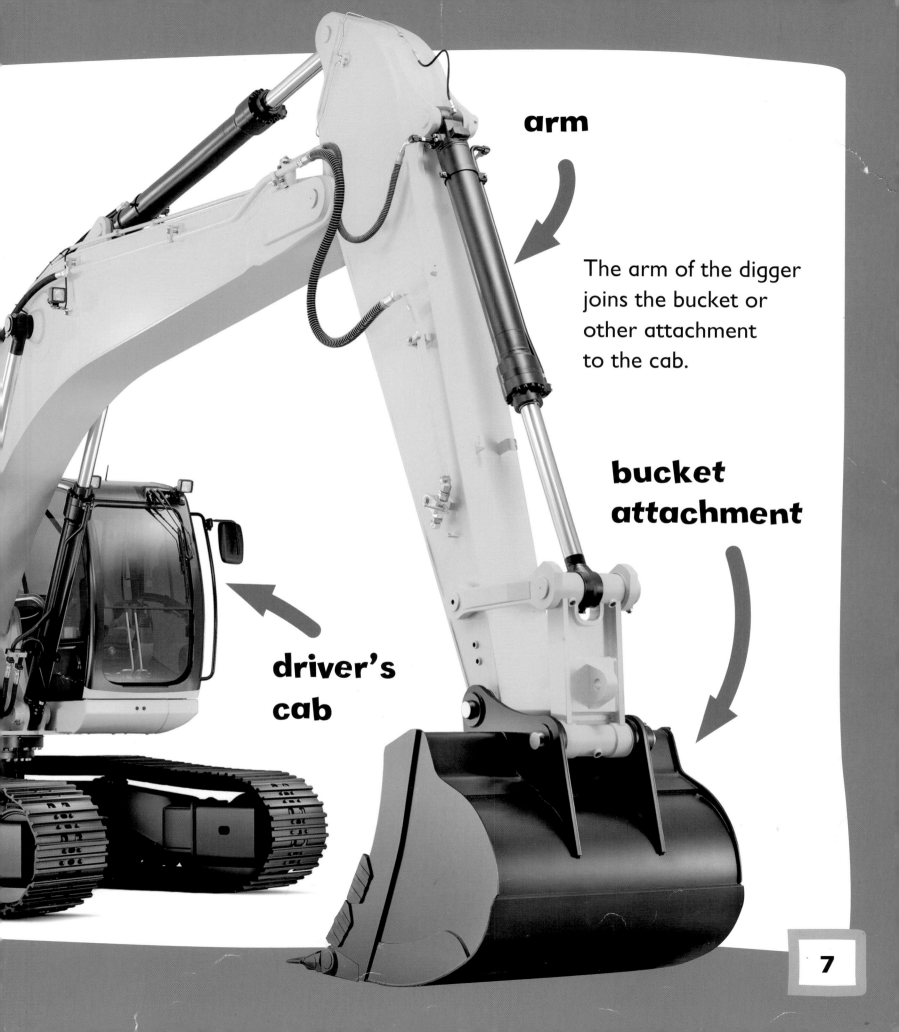

arm

The arm of the digger joins the bucket or other attachment to the cab.

bucket attachment

driver's cab

7

Buckets

The bucket is at the end of the arm. Buckets are made of metal and come in many shapes and sizes. Each one does a different job.

The teeth on a bucket are large, but not sharp. They push through the ground, just like your teeth bite into food.

teeth

Some buckets are very wide. The driver uses a wide bucket to scrape up earth or stones.

A wide bucket collects lots of stones in each scoop.

Digging and moving

The digger is one of the most important machines on a building site. It digs up the ground and clears away any unwanted **rubble**.

grab

The grab clamps together to lift and hold the rubble.

A grab is like two buckets that bite together. A grab is used to lift and carry heavy objects, such as piles of rocks.

This excavator is digging a trench for water pipes.

Breaking up
hard ground

Diggers can break through almost any ground, even frozen earth. This means that building work can carry on in almost any weather!

The spike has to hit the ground over and over again to break up hard earth.

A ripper is used instead of a bucket. When the ripper crashes into the hard surface, it makes the ground crack.

A ripper is a spike that is shaped like the letter V.

ripper

Demolition

Excavators can be used to knock down houses and small office blocks. This is called demolition. Excavators **demolish** a building safely, bit by bit.

Some diggers can reach up to 328 feet (100 meters) in height —that's as tall as the Statue of Liberty.

An excavator can demolish tall buildings, too. It has a very long arm that can reach up to the top of the building.

The excavator's driver controls which way the building falls down.

Sucking up waste

A suction excavator has a special **hose** to suck up waste. It can be used to remove soil from a hole, or water from a river or a swimming pool.

A suction excavator is useful for cleaning **sewage pipes**. It can also clean up river banks without scraping away any of the land.

A suction excavator works fast. The hose could empty a bathtub in only four minutes!

This machine works like a vacuum cleaner to suck up waste into the truck.

Mining

Excavators are used in **mining**, especially to remove **coal**. This kind of excavator is called a dragline excavator, because the bucket is dragged along the ground.

bucket

The bucket is moved by steel ropes. One of the ropes moves the bucket up and down. Other ropes move it from side to side.

steel ropes

arm

utility
coals (1978) ltd.

195-B

Biggest and smallest

The biggest excavator in the world works in coal mines. It is called Bagger 288 and it weighs 50,150 tons (45,500 tonnes)— the same weight as 550 passenger planes.

This monster machine can move 265,000 tons (240,000 tonnes) of coal a day. This is the same weight as 40,000 elephants or 3,000 passenger planes.

There are many mini—excavators. They are used in yards to clear yard waste or for small building jobs.

This is one of the smallest mini-excavators!

Activities

- Can you name these three attachments from the book? Can you remember what each one does?

- An excavator can knock down a building. Why is it a good machine to use?

- Draw a building site with as many diggers as you could use. Which ones did you choose? What color are they?

- Which picture shows a suction excavator?

Glossary

Attachment
A tool on the end of a digger's arm. The tool is usually a bucket.

Bucket
A large container on the end of a digger's arm. It is used to scoop up earth and stones.

Building site
A place where a house or other building is being built.

Bulldozer
A tractor with a blade on the front. It is used to push earth and rubble.

Coal
A hard, black rock that is dug out of the ground. We burn it mainly to make electricity.

Demolish
To knock down a building.

Hose
A long pipe or tube.

Loader
A tractor with a large bucket on the front.

Mining
Taking coal out of the ground.

Rubble
Broken stones or bricks, usually on a building site.

Sewage pipe
A pipe that takes away waste from people's homes and offices.

Index

3 1901 05379 3099